Pepper Spray in Paradise

Paul Davenport

Pepper Spray in Paradise

Ernst Klett Sprachen
Stuttgart

1. Auflage 1 10 9 8 7 6 | 2021 20 19 18 17

Internetadresse: www.klett-sprachen.de

Redaktion: Paul Newcomb
Layoutkonzeption: Elmar Feuerbach
Gestaltung und Satz: Swabianmedia, Stuttgart
Umschlaggestaltung: Elmar Feuerbach
Titelbild: iStockphoto (floridastock), Calgary, Alberta
Druck und Bindung: CEWE Stiftung & Co. KGaA, Germering
Printed in Germany

ISBN 978-3-12-542602-3

9 783125 426023

Contents

Introduction / About the author 6

Maps of the area 7

Quiz 9

Pepper Spray in Paradise 10

Solutions to the Quiz 48

Bildquellenverzeichnis

S. 6: Paul Davenport, Lingen; S. 7: Fotosearch Stock Photography (Digital Wisdom), Waukesha, WI; S. 8: USDA - U.S. Department of Agriculture - PD, Washington; S. 10; S. 20: shutterstock (Zack Frank), New York, NY; S. 31: iStockphoto (Babu Rangasamy), Calgary, Alberta; S. 36: Corbis (Steve Terrill), Düsseldorf; S. 42: Getty Images (Nat. Geographic/ Medford Taylor), München;

Nicht in allen Fällen war es uns möglich, den Rechteinhaber der Abbildungen ausfindig zu machen. Berechtigte Ansprüche werden selbst-verständlich im Rahmen der üblichen Vereinbarungen abgegolten.

Abbreviations used in annotations

in	finformal
sb	somebody
sth	something

About the book

Pepper Spray in Paradise is a story about Josh, a city boy from New Jersey, who because of his mother's health problems, has to move to a small town in New Hampshire, in the middle of the White Mountain National Forest. Gradually, he overcomes his homesickness as he discovers the fascination of the WMNF.

It's a beautiful place but what he doesn't realize at first – it can be a very dangerous place, especially for a guy like himself, who doesn't look the other way when he sees visitors break the park rules.

About the author

Part of the White Mountain National Forest is in Maine, the state Paul Davenport grew up in. Like Josh, the main character of *Pepper Spray in Paradise*, he loves the Great Outdoors, having spent many happy hours of his youth in the woods. (Unlike Josh, he usually had a fishing pole with him.)

Not long after graduating from college with a major in English, he and his German wife moved to Germany, to the city of Lingen, where they brought up three sons.

The roots of his writing career go back to the stage plays he wrote for his English classes. One year, he submitted one of his plays to a publisher and thus *The Royal Choice* (1996) became his first publication! Four years later, he wrote the first of several school readers and hasn't stopped writing since.

A highlight in his writing career has been the nomination of two readers as finalists in the Extensive Reading Foundation's annual competition for reader of the year. *Crossroads to Love* was a finalist in 2007, and in 2008 *Horror Trip on the Pecos River* even won the coveted first prize.

Paul reads a lot of modern fiction, especially detective stories (his favorite is the Harry Bosch series by Michael Connelly). He also enjoys fishing and playing table tennis.

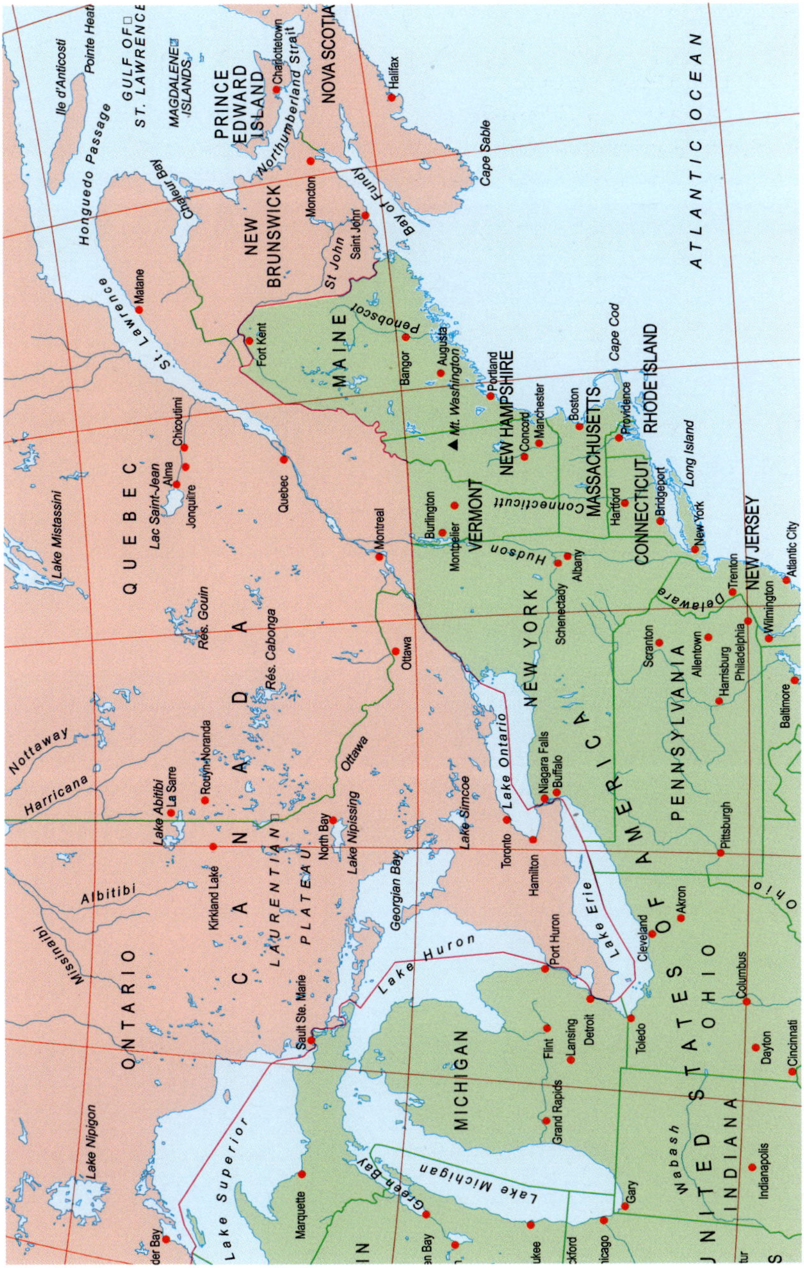

ATLANTIC OCEAN
GULF OF ST. LAWRENCE
Ile d'Anticosti
Pointe Heath
Honguedo Passage
MAGDALENE ISLANDS
PRINCE EDWARD ISLAND
Charlottetown
Northumberland Strait
NOVA SCOTIA
Halifax
Cape Sable
Chaleur Bay
NEW BRUNSWICK
Moncton
Saint John
St John
Bay of Fundy
St. Lawrence
Matane
Fort Kent
MAINE
Penobscot
Bangor
Augusta
Mt. Washington
Portland
NEW HAMPSHIRE
Concord
Manchester
Boston
MASSACHUSETTS
Cape Cod
Providence
RHODE ISLAND
Long Island
CONNECTICUT
Hartford
Bridgeport
Connecticut
VERMONT
Burlington
Montpelier
Hudson
Albany
Schenectady
NEW YORK
New York
NEW JERSEY
Trenton
Atlantic City
Delaware
Wilmington
Philadelphia
Allentown
Scranton
Harrisburg
Baltimore
PENNSYLVANIA
Pittsburgh
Ohio
QUEBEC
Lac Saint-Jean
Alma
Chicoutimi
Jonquière
Quebec
Montreal
Lake Mistassini
Rés. Gouin
Rés. Cabonga
Ottawa
CANADA
Nottaway
Harricana
Lake Abitibi
La Sarre
Rouyn-Noranda
Kirkland Lake
Albitibi
Missinaibi
LAURENTIAN PLATEAU
North Bay
Lake Nipissing
Georgian Bay
Lake Simcoe
Toronto
Hamilton
Lake Ontario
Niagara Falls
Buffalo
Lake Erie
ONTARIO
Sault Ste. Marie
Lake Huron
Port Huron
Detroit
Toledo
Cleveland
Akron
Columbus
Dayton
Cincinnati
OHIO
UNITED STATES OF AMERICA
MICHIGAN
Flint
Lansing
Grand Rapids
Lake Michigan
Green Bay
Gary
Wabash
INDIANA
Indianapolis
Lake Superior
Marquette
Lake Nipigon

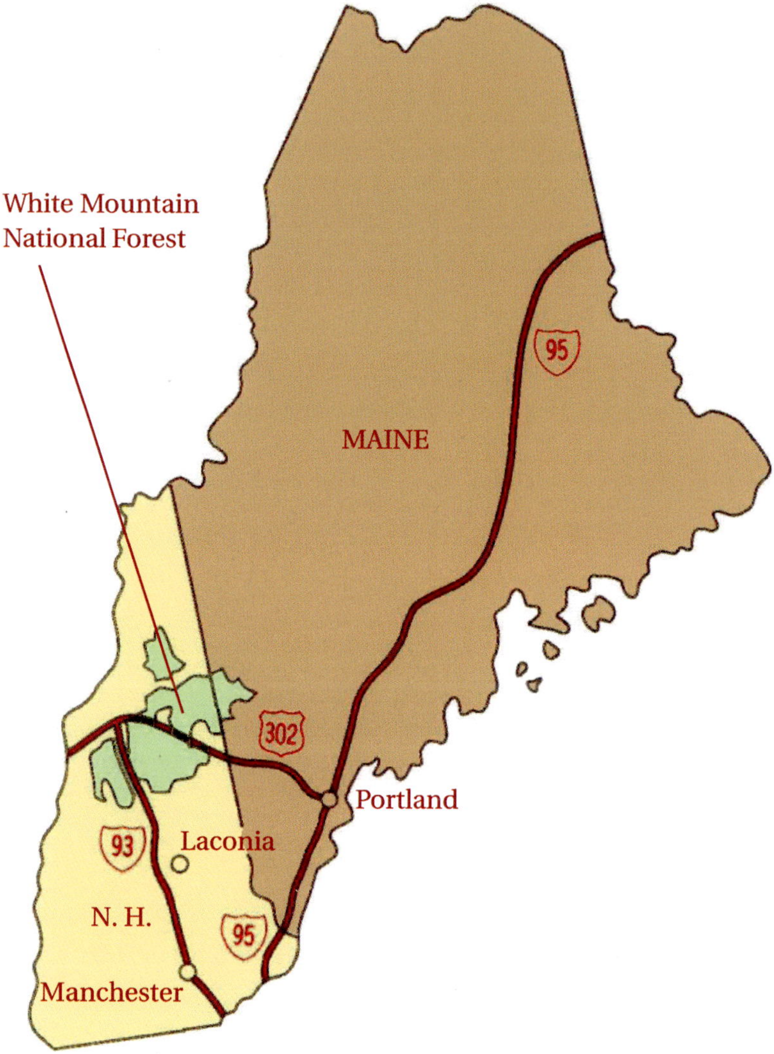
White Mountain
National Forest
MAINE
95
302
Portland
93
Laconia
N. H.
95
Manchester

Quiz

Use the internet to find the answers to these quiz questions. *Answers are on page 48.*

1 How far is it from New Union, New Jersey, to New York City?

2 How far is it from New Union to Glen, New Hampshire?

3 How large is the White Mountain National Forest (WMNF)?

4 What is the name of the park's highest mountain? How high is it?

5 Name at least ten wild animals which can be found in the WMNF.

6 How many visitors a year come to the WMNF?

7 How many campsites are there in the WMNF?

8 Where does the Appalachian Trail start and end?

9 How long is the Appalachian Trail?

10 How many miles of trails are there in the WMNF?

11 How many miles of the Appalachian Trail run through the WMNF?

12 Strictly speaking, the WMNF is a national forest, not a national park. How many national forests are there in the U.S.A.?

13 What is the difference between a national forest and a national park?

1

Josh wasn't happy when his mom said they were moving. He liked his hometown of New Union, New Jersey, very much, thank you. He really felt at home there. The only problem was the air. It was so close to New York City that it got a lot of the bad air coming from there. And, he knew, it was bad air that was making Gloria, his mother, sick. The doctor had said that she should move to where the air was clean. But hey! Glen? Population 4,523. In northern New Hampshire? In the middle of a national park, the White Mountain National Forest? You must be kidding!

When he realized that his mom had made up her mind and the move was coming whether he liked it or not, he had done some quick research on New Hampshire on the Internet. He thought that he might as well learn something about the state he'd be living in.

10 **to make up your mind** to decide

He had found some interesting things. For example, Native Americans had lived there for over three thousand years (!) before the 'white man' came from Europe and settled there in 1623. And, for the next 150 years New Hampshire was a British colony. But in 1776 – and that surprised Josh and made him a little proud - New Hampshire became independent, becoming the first state of the United States! Also, in the same year, it was New Hampshire, as the only independent state along with twelve British colonies, that declared independence from Britain!

(Josh had learned that the state's main industry, the textile industry, had been important in the past, but by the 1930s strong competition from southern states had meant the end of that once proud industry. At the same time, farming was failing, too. Things were looking bad. The population of the state went from one million down to 600,000. But then came World War II and New Hampshire became the nation's builder of submarines. And after the war, tourism began to boom and has since become the most important part of the state's economy.)

Josh also learned a little about the geography of New Hampshire. Like New Jersey, it was one of the smallest states in the US, with a total area of 9,300 square miles, making it about the size of countries like Qatar or Belgium. But though it was not much larger than New Jersey, one of the biggest differences between his home state and New Hampshire was the size of the population. With 8.7 million people to 1.3 million, New Jersey had almost seven times more people than New Hampshire! Josh didn't like that idea. He didn't feel good about living in a place with so few people.

But okay, it was all about his mother, not about him. Maybe, when she was feeling well again, they could move back to New Union. Or at least to another city in New Jersey. For now, he had to accept his fate. His mom was happy. Not only was the air clean in Glen, she had found a new job there working at the Glen Visitor Information Center. The bad thing about Glen was, Josh didn't know what to do. The kids his age in Glen were - well, different - from the kids he had known in New Union. Different? It was like they came from another

16 **submarine** boat that travels under the surface of the water – 31 **fate** [feɪt] the bad or unfortunate thing(s) that had happened to him

planet! How did they spend their time? Fishing, hunting, swimming and hanging around. Mainly hanging around, the boys watching the girls and the girls watching the boys. It wasn't Josh's world. And he wasn't interested in making it his world.

The world of Josh Davis was different. An important part of it was photography. He had hundreds of photos stored in his computer. Of his classmates, his clique, his baseball team, of everything. Pictures of his happy days in New Union.

What, he asked himself, would he take pictures of now? In Glen? His first few weeks there had been a bad time. He had never felt so bored in all his life. Finally, not knowing what to do with himself, he started taking walks, something he had almost never done before. He wanted to be alone. And where could he better be alone than in the White Mountain National Forest? At first he didn't like it there. It felt – strange. Kind of scary. Everything was so quiet. But after a week or so he began to get used to the quiet. In fact, he soon found to his surprise that he even liked it. After that, it became his routine. As soon as school was out, he went straight home, had a quick bite to eat, and headed off to the park.

Not only did he enjoy being in the forest, he soon began to notice things he would like to take pictures of: the mountains, the streams, and - most of all - the wild animals. The park was full of wild animals. He started taking his camera with him when he went on his walks.

He didn't get good pictures right from the start. In the beginning, he made the same mistake most amateur photographers make. When they see wild animals they get nervous. Instead of waiting for the right moment, they start taking photos at once. The result is, they frighten the animals or birds away. Josh had to learn how to wait. He had to learn that the way to get a good picture was to be very still and quiet. It was only then that wild animals came close enough for a good photo. He came to realize that wild animals really are WILD animals. They have learned to be careful. If they are not sure whether a newcomer is dangerous or not, they don't wait around to find out. They run away. The only way they're going to stay around is if they feel safe in the newcomer's presence.

7 **clique** [kli:k] group of friends that is together a lot

His mother wasn't happy about him spending so much time in the park. She worried about him. She had this idea that it was full of wild animals and - she said this ten times a day - some of them were DANGEROUS. There were moose, coyotes and BEARS, she said, always in that order, always almost shouting the word 'bears'. As if the bears were all hungry and just waiting for the next human to come along!

'Don't go too far, Josh.' 'Don't stay away too long, Josh.' 'Don't get off the path, Josh.' 'Don't get near any DANGEROUS ANIMALS, Josh.' She made him feel like he was entering the deepest jungle in Africa!

Okay, he knew he had to be careful. And yes, he was only thirteen years old and an only child. He could understand why she worried so much about him. But he wished that she would trust him more.

4 **moose** large deer that lives in North America (called an *elk* in Europe)

2

In the weeks that followed, Josh came to feel more and more at home in The Whites, as the White Mountain National Forest was called. (His name for it was simply paradise.) But he didn't want his mother to worry about him so he always told her where he was going, what trails he would be on, and when he was coming back. This, and the fact that he always had his cell phone with him, made her feel better. It made him feel better, too.

In those first weeks he took a large number of photos. He had come upon a colony of beavers, busy building their houses. He returned to 'Beaver City' again and again, and got some very good pictures. He had also got several photos of deer, which was easy. You weren't allowed to hunt them in the White Mountain National Forest, so they were everywhere.

But Josh wanted to take photos of the more unusual animals in the park. When he asked a ranger where he could get a picture of a moose, he was told that the best place to find one was over in the Bridge Lake area. It took Josh over an hour to walk there but it was worth it. When he looked out across the lake his heart took a jump. There, on the other side, stood a mother moose with her two calves!

It took Josh another half hour to get near enough for a good photo. He was careful not to get too close. He had heard about how dangerous moose mothers could be when you got too near their calves.

He waited for the right moment - the moose had just pulled her head out of the water - then pressed the button. At the loud CLICK of the camera the mother moose turned her head and stared in Josh's direction. And stared some more. Josh held his breath, his heart started making loud noises and his legs began to shake. He got ready to run. A moment which seemed as long as an hour went by. Finally, the moose put her head underwater again. Josh breathed out slowly. Then he turned, and walking as quietly as possible, put distance between himself and the moose. When he was on the other side of the lake, he looked back. The mother moose and her two calves were gone. He smiled. He had them in his camera!

5 **trail** [treɪl] route of paths which you can follow on a hike (long walk)

Meanwhile, spring had turned to summer and more and more tourists were coming to The Whites. Josh felt good when he saw their happy faces, especially those of the children. He knew how good it was for children to be out in the forest, away from television, computers and video games. In touch with nature.

What he didn't feel so good about were the tourists who didn't follow the park rules. Especially the rule about respecting wild animals. While most campers and hikers behaved well, there were a few who treated the forest like a zoo or an amusement park, and not like the paradise it was. And the bad thing was, they didn't have to worry about being caught. Everyone knew about the situation in America's national parks. There were far too few rangers to go around. At a time when the number of people visiting the parks was growing, government funding had been cut back and the parks were forced to reduce its staff of park rangers.

Josh saw the results everywhere: hikers who had gone off the trails, campers who were camping far from the legal sites and, worst of all, off-road vehicles driving through areas where they weren't allowed to drive! Not only did the ORVs pollute the water and air, they also tore up the land. These powerful vehicles were like an invading army, shattering the peace and quiet of nature and driving off the animals.

A feeling had been growing in Josh that he couldn't just stand by and let this happen. He had come to believe that he had to do something about it, and he began to think of himself as a kind of assistant ranger. Whenever he saw off-limits hikers or campers, he reminded them of the park rules. Of course, they didn't always thank him for this. In fact, they sometimes became angry and aggressive. But he didn't let that stop him. And when he saw ORVs where they weren't allowed to be, he called the Ranger Station and reported it. Unfortunately, there wasn't always someone on duty at the station, and if there was they often said that there were no rangers in the

8 **hiker** ['haɪkɚ] person that goes for long walks in the country – 17 **site** campsite: place where people camp in tents for their vacation – 19 **ORV** off-road vehicle: motor bike, car or truck that you can drive on trails or through forests (if you are allowed!) – 21 **to shatter** to destroy, break, ruin – 26 **off-limits** if you are off-limits, you are where you are not allowed to be

area Josh was reporting from. But once in a while Josh got lucky and a ranger was sent to deal with the problem.

Times had changed since 9 -11, Josh knew. American society had grown more violent, less safe. Life for park rangers had changed, too. Not only were there too few of them, their job had become even more dangerous. In the years following 9 -11 many rangers had been attacked, some even killed. The national parks were being misused, sometimes as a route for illegal immigrants, sometimes as a place to grow marijuana. It was a good thing, Josh thought, that the rangers were now getting self-defense training and were allowed to use pepper spray.

Maybe he should get some training in self-defense, too, he thought.

2 **to deal with** to solve (a problem)

3

On the July 4th weekend Josh stayed at home. His mom had planned a barbeque and invited the neighbors. She wanted him to meet the neighbors, too. And she needed his help with the preparations. Another good reason for staying at home was that on this weekend the park was overcrowded with tourists. He had read somewhere that the White Mountain National Forest had more visitors annually than Yellowstone and Yosemite combined! From his backyard Josh could see the endless line of cars moving slowly through Glen, on their way into the park. He thought of the rangers, what a difficult time it would be for them. He also thought of the wild animals and felt sorry for them. It would be a noisy and stressful weekend for them.

On Monday morning, Josh was back in the park. Most of the holiday tourists were gone but, as usual, signs of their visit were everywhere: cartons, bottles, cans, old newspapers, even pieces of clothing! When Josh had first started coming to the park, he had hardly noticed these things. But all that had changed and he had become painfully aware of the damage tourists did to the park. The litter they left behind not only spoiled the beautiful landscape, it was also a danger to the animals. Especially broken glass the animals might step on, or half-empty plastic yogurt cartons animals might try to eat.

But litter wasn't the biggest problem. Litter could be cleaned up. There were other things visitors did which he couldn't do much about: the graffiti on the rocks, the names cut into the trees, the stolen signs, etc. Where was the respect for nature, he asked himself, and shook his head sadly.

There was one thing he was thankful for: the noise that had filled the park on the weekend was gone. Josh stopped what he was doing for a moment, lifted his face to the sun and closed his eyes. He smiled as he breathed in the cool air and listened to the quiet sounds of the forest. Suddenly, PING! PING! PING! His eyes opened wide at the sound of BB guns. Then he heard laughter. Boys laughing. He moved quickly along the trail in the direction the noise was coming from. With each step his anger grew. As he came to a bend he slowed down. The laughter was very loud now. Then he saw them: three

17 **painfully** extremely – 18 **litter** rubbish, trash, waste material – 32 **BB gun** air gun that shoots tiny bullets (pellets)

boys, about 14 or 15 years old, Josh thought. They were shooting at something in a tree. He moved closer.

He was careful not to make any noise. When he reached a rock not far from them, he looked out and caught sight of what they were shooting at. There, near the top of a tall tree, its beautiful red-brown fur shining in the sun, was a squirrel. It was jumping from branch to branch. *Keep going little guy*, Josh thought, *don't let them get you!* But the three boys kept shooting at it and when it stopped for a moment to look around, one of them hit it. For several seconds, the squirrel hung from the branch it was on, then fell to the ground. The boys ran over to where it lay, laughing wildly.

Josh came out from behind the rock and walked over to them. They didn't see him until he was standing right behind them.

'Hey,' said the biggest boy, 'what do you want?'

Josh didn't answer. He got up closer and looked at the dead squirrel. There was a hole where its eye had been. For a long moment, Josh just stood there and said nothing. Surprised at Josh's cool reaction, the three boys looked at one another. Finally, the biggest boy said again, louder this time, 'What do you want?'

Josh turned to face him slowly, as if coming out of a dream. 'You killed this squirrel,' he said softly. 'What are you doing in the park with BB guns? You know that that's not allowed!'

The boys looked at each other and broke into laughter. Then they raised their guns and did a little Indian dance around Josh. When they stopped, the biggest boy stepped up right into Josh's face. 'What are we doing?' he cried. 'You saw what we're doing. We're getting ourselves some squirrel meat.' This was followed by more dancing and wild laughter.

Josh ignored them. He was looking at the dead squirrel. When they noticed this, they stopped their dance. Slowly, Josh turned to face them. 'Killing a little animal like this – how does it make you feel? Does it make you feel big and strong?'

The boys stopped grinning and turned their eyes away.

'I could report you for this, you know. That would mean big trouble,' Josh said. 'But if you leave the park now, I'll forget about what I've seen here.'

6 **squirrel** ['skwɜːrl] small animal with a bushy tail which can be gray or reddish-brown

One of the boys turned to the biggest boy and said in a mock-serious voice, 'That's very kind of our friend here, don't you think, Ryan?'

Ryan, playing along, nodded his head slowly. 'Oh, yes.' He turned to the third boy. 'What do you think of our friend's suggestion, Billy?'

Billy nodded, too. 'Good. Very good. But I think we should thank him before we go.' He gave Ryan a knowing smile.

'Right,' said Ryan. Suddenly, his voice turned cold. 'Listen, you little smart-ass. Pick up your squirrel, put it in your bag, and get the hell out of here before we start shooting at you!'

Josh didn't move, he just stood there and stared at him. Ryan got nervous. For a moment, he didn't know what to do. Then, suddenly, he pushed his gun into Josh's face. 'YOU HEARD ME! TAKE YOUR SQUIRREL AND GET TO HELL OUT OF HERE!'

Josh still didn't move. He continued to stare into Ryan's eyes.

'I've got an idea. Let's see if our friend can dance,' Billy said with a big smile.

'Good idea!' Ryan said. He took a step back and aimed his gun at the ground next to Josh's feet.

'I'm not going to dance,' Josh said calmly, looking Ryan straight in the eye. 'But if you shoot that gun again, you're going to be in deep trouble. This is your last chance. Leave now and I'll forget about this. Keep acting stupid and I'll report you.'

Ryan's mouth fell open. He looked at the other two boys. They were just as surprised as he was. For the next long moment, he stared at Josh, trying to think of a way to make him leave. Josh stared back. Finally, Ryan forced a laugh. 'Okay, this time we'll let you go, but if we ever see you here again you'd better run for your life!'

'Oh shit, Ryan. We want to see him dance,' said Billy.

'Yeah, come on, Ryan,' said the other boy.

'Shut up you two and do what I say! Get moving! We've got better things to do than stand around here talking with a squirrel-lover!'

Josh watched them as they walked away. Suddenly, he noticed that his knees were shaking. He let out his breath slowly and smiled. He had won.

1 **mock-serious** not really serious (i.e. pretending to be serious) – 9 **smart-ass** ['sma:rtæs] *(inf)* rude word for sb who you think is trying to be clever (or is actually cleverer than you) –

4

On the Saturday before the beginning of the new school year Josh got up early. His mother liked to sleep late Saturdays and was still in bed. He had told her that he was going to spend the morning in the park. He would be back for dinner, he said.

Josh left the house immediately after breakfast and hurried to the park. It had rained a lot the past few days so he was wearing his rubber boots. Within an hour he had reached Baker's Pond, his first stop of the morning. There he took a few photos of a family of ducks before moving on. They were swimming in the usual formation, mother duck at the head of the family, the baby ducks behind her. There were six of them, so small that Josh was surprised that they could already swim so well.

The weather was sunny but with a cool breeze that grew cooler further into the forest. He was on a little-known trail, one that tourists hardly ever used. As he walked along, he listened for unusual birdcalls. He already had a large collection of bird photos but today he was looking for birds he hadn't yet photographed.

When he reached Little Joe's Stream an hour later, he stopped for a rest. He took a sandwich and a bottle of chocolate milk out of his backpack. He opened the sandwich and inspected it. Mm. Peanut butter and strawberry jelly, his favorite. He had just taken his first bite when he heard loud voices. Surprised, he held his breath and listened. They were coming from somewhere off to his right. He put his sandwich and milk down and started in the direction the voices were coming from. As he got closer, the voices grew louder and so did his heart.

Even before he saw them, he knew that it was two angry men shouting at each other. They were standing beside their ATVs. One of them was stuck in deep mud.

Josh hid behind a bush and listened.

'You should have listened to me. I told you that we should have left the ATVs on the trail,' the older of the two said.

'Come on, Russ, face the facts! You followed me in here and - you got stuck. Instead of driving around the mud hole like I said, you had to try to go right through it!' the younger man said. He was wearing jeans and a dark-colored sweatshirt.

'How could I know it was this deep?'

'You didn't have to test it!' the younger man said. 'It's a good thing one of us has some common sense.'

'Ha! Whose idea was it to leave the trail and go off through the woods? "We can drive straight to the stream," you said.' The older man's voice was angry. 'Just so you wouldn't have to walk a few minutes.'

'You didn't have to follow me.'

Josh shook his head angrily. Instead of parking on the trail and going by foot to the stream, which was only a five-minute walk from the trail, they had left the ORV trail and driven through the woods. Josh took out his cell phone and dialed the Ranger Station. He held

6 **backpack** American word for *rucksack* – 14 **ATV** all-terrain vehicle: a vehicle that can drive over rough ground (or indeed any ground) as well as roads – 25 **common sense** the ability to think sensibly and in a practical way

his breath while the phone rang. Please, he said to himself, let there be someone there! He waited several seconds, but there was no answer. When he closed his cell, a bird let out a loud call and flew up from the tree beside him.

'HEY YOU! COME OVER HERE!' They had seen him. Josh put his cell phone away quickly and stepped out from behind the bush.

'Hi,' he said, putting on a friendly smile. 'Can I help?'

The two men looked him up and down. 'You?' said the younger man with a twisted grin. 'How could you help us?'

'I'm stronger than I look,' Josh said, trying to keep the fear out of his voice.

Both of them laughed wildly. 'We don't need any help,' the younger man said. He reached into a box on his ATV and pulled out a chain. He looked at the man called Russ and smiled. 'I'll have you out in no time,' he said. Turning to Josh, he said, 'Stand back, kid, and watch this.'

The younger man fixed the chain onto the front of the other ATV, then got onto his own and started the motor. He stepped on the gas and his ATV jumped forward. When the other ATV didn't move at first, he stepped harder on the gas. Finally, it began to move slowly forward. A moment later, it was out of the hole. The younger man laughed as he put the chain back. He turned to Josh with a didn't-I-tell-you look on his grinning face.

There was a flash of anger in Josh's eyes. 'You guys are off limits here. You'd better get back to the trail quickly,' he said. 'Before the ranger comes.'

'Ranger? What ranger?' said Russ.

'The one they sent after you,' said Josh with a straight face.

'Did you hear that? Vinnie. The little man has called the rangers.' Both men began to laugh.

'What's so funny?' Josh asked.

Vinnie looked Josh in the eye and said, 'When we drove by the station a little while ago, there was a big sign on the door. Guess what it said!'

'I - I don't know,' Josh said.

'Closed till 1 o'clock.' There was a winner's smile on Vinnie's face.

He was staring at Josh. Suddenly, his eyes turned cold. 'We don't like it when people try to trick us, especially smart-ass kids like you,' he said. 'What's your name, boy?'

'Josh.'

'Well, Josh. I think we'll have to teach you a lesson. About not sticking your nose into other people's business. First of all, give us that cell phone in your back pocket.'

Josh turned to run but Vinnie was faster. He grabbed the boy and pulled him down. The next moment, he had the cell phone in his hand. 'What are we going to do with this phone, Russ?' He handed Russ the phone.

Russ turned it over in his hand. 'Too bad to throw away a really expensive phone like this.'

Josh reached out to get his phone back but Vinnie held him tight. He laughed. 'You'd like to have your phone back, wouldn't you? Well, you can't. You've been a bad boy.'

'You can look at it this way,' said Russ, poker-faced. 'Without a cell phone, you won't have to pay all that money to the telephone company every month. You should be thankful to us.' With a wild laugh Russ turned and threw the phone in the stream.

'Okay. Now we want to have a look at that backpack. What have you got in there?' Vinnie held out his hand.

'Nothing. I had some sandwiches but I ate them,' Josh said.

'Gimme!'

Josh took a step back.

'Either you give me that backpack or I take it! You have a choice.' Vinnie continued to hold out his hand.

Slowly, Josh took off his backpack and handed it over.

'Hey!' Vinnie said as he opened it and saw the camera. 'What have we got here?' He eyed Josh suspiciously. 'You didn't take any pictures of us, did you?'

'No, I didn't.'

Vinnie opened the camera. 'I believe you but just to make sure, I'll remove this chip.'

'Please don't! There are only photos of wild animals on it!'

17 **poker-faced** showing no thoughts or feelings – 30 **suspiciously** [sə'spɪʃəsli] in a way that shows you don't trust sb

'We can't take any chances. Sorry about that.' He took out the chip and put it in his pocket.

Josh was wild with anger but he held himself back. There was nothing he could do against two grown men. He just stared at Vinnie.

'And now,' Vinnie said slowly with a wide grin, 'we're going to take you for a little ride.'

'You won't get away with this,' Josh said in an angry voice.

The two men looked at each other and started laughing. When they finally stopped, Russ told Josh to sit down behind him on the ATV and hold on. As soon as he did, Russ started off and headed up the hill next to the stream. Josh thought about jumping off but he could hear the other ATV right behind them and knew that Vinnie was watching him closely.

When they reached the top of the hill, Russ stopped and turned off the motor. 'End of the line. Get off!' he said, turning around.

Josh looked at him helplessly. 'You're not going to leave me here, are you?'

Russ laughed. 'The walk back will do you good. And it'll give you time to think about what we told you.'

'About minding your own business,' Vinnie said with a cruel laugh. 'Maybe you'll think twice before you do something like that again.'

'Please. I - '

But before Josh could finish, Russ had started the motor. Suddenly, Josh jumped onto the seat behind him. In a flash, Vinnie got off his ATV and pushed Josh hard to the ground. Before the boy could get up, the two men were on their way down the hill.

Josh picked himself up slowly. He watched the ATVs as they raced down the hill and out of sight. Suddenly, he noticed that he was cold. Cold and - without his cell phone - very much alone. For a moment, he felt like crying. In fact, several tears rolled down his face. He had never felt so - helpless - in his whole life.

21 **to mind your own business** to concentrate on your own affairs and not ask questions about others

5

It took Josh more than an hour to find his way back to the trail, and another hour to reach the Ranger Station. He was happy when he saw the White Forest National Park SUV parked in front of the station.

'What happened to you?' said Ranger Scott Logan when Josh came through the door. 'You didn't meet up with a bear, did you?' Josh knew Ranger Logan and liked him. He had met him on one of his first visits to the park and often stopped in at the station to talk with him. Ranger Logan liked Josh, too, and was impressed by his strong interest in the park. He always enjoyed talking with him.

'Not with a bear. With two men. They drove their ATVs through the woods over at Little Joe's Stream. When I told them they were off limits, they got angry and took me up a hill and left me there.'

Logan's eyes were open wide. 'But Josh, why didn't you call the station and report them?'

'I did - as soon as I saw them. But that was before you opened up. After that, when they caught me, they took my cell phone away from me.'

'Too bad I wasn't at the station. I was at a meeting in Redstone all morning,' Logan said. 'Come on in to my office, Josh, and sit down. That was a hell of a long walk.' The ranger led Josh into his office and pointed to a chair. 'You must be hungry. How about a sandwich and some coffee to wash it down with?'

Josh smiled. 'I don't usually drink coffee.'

'It'll do you good.' Logan handed him a sandwich and poured him a cup of coffee. He waited a few minutes while Josh ate and drank before he spoke again. 'Tell me some more about your friends on the ATVs,' he said.

Josh had to smile at the word 'friends'. 'Right. Their names are Russ and Vinnie. Russ is an older guy, around 50, I'd say. Vinnie is about 25, 30 at the most. Their plan was to fish Little Joe's Stream but they were too lazy to walk. So instead of parking their vehicles on the trail, they decided to drive right to the stream. That's where I met up with them, near the stream. I was sitting there resting when

3 **SUV** sports utility vehicle: a car that has space for sports equipment and often has four-wheel drive for rough roads – 15 **to report** if you report sb, you say to sb in authority that they have done something wrong

I heard them. The older man had got his ATV stuck in a mud hole. That's when I tried to call you.'

'What happened after that?'

Ranger Logan listened quietly while Josh told his story. When Josh came to the part about the men leaving him on top of the hill, the ranger shook his head. 'And you walked – all the way back to the station?' he said.

'Yeah.'

Logan smiled at Josh. 'You must be tired. I'll take you home.'

'What about the two men?' Josh's eyes flashed with anger.

'Oh, I'll have a look for them afterwards but I want to get you home first. Your mom will be worried about you, won't she?'

'Not really. I'll call her. But - if it's all right with you, I'd like to go with you and help you find the men.'

Surprised, Logan hesitated. His eyes studied Josh's face for a long moment. Finally, he said, 'Let's see what your mother says first.' He handed the telephone to the boy.

Josh dialed quickly. 'Mom, it's me, Josh…At the Ranger Station… Not yet, Mom. Ranger Logan wants me to help him with something… Okay, Mom…Yeah, by five o'clock. I promise…Bye.'

Logan shook his head - and smiled.

15 **to hesitate** to stop for a moment because you are unsure

6

'There it is up ahead,' Josh said.

After he had parked his SUV beside the trail, Logan had followed Josh through the woods. A moment later, they were standing beside the mud hole Russ's ATV had got stuck in. Logan studied the wheel marks around the hole, then walked over to the place where the ATVs had come through the woods. He shook his head. 'Look at the ground here,' he said to Josh. 'Look at how they tore it up! It'll take years for this to grow back!' Logan's voice was sad - and angry.

'I know,' Josh said.

For a long second, Logan continued to stare at the damage done by the ATVs. Then he went back to the mud hole and looked around. 'We've got to find those men,' he said in an angry voice.

'I just thought of something,' Josh said. 'I could see quite a bit of the stream from the top of the hill. Maybe we can spot them from there.'

'Good idea.' Logan turned and looked at the hill. 'It's easy to see where they drove up.' Without saying another word, he started up the hill. Josh hurried to catch up with him.

They didn't say much on their way up. When they reached the top, they turned around and looked down. Below them lay a long stretch of Little Joe's Stream. Logan was the first one to spot the men. 'There they are!' he cried. 'Do you see them?' He pointed down the hill and to the left.

'Yeah! That's them!' Josh said. 'I can recognize - ' But Logan didn't wait for Josh to finish. He was already moving quickly down the hill.

'Let me do the talking,' Logan said to Josh when they reached the stream. From where they stood, behind some trees, they could see the two men in the middle of the stream fishing. Logan, followed by Josh, walked slowly out of the woods and stood quietly beside the stream. When the men saw the two of them, they talked with each other quickly before they started coming towards them. Josh had to look twice when he saw how Russ was moving - dragging one leg in the water behind him like Frankenstein! *What's this all about?* Josh thought and almost had to laugh.

Russ was the first to speak. 'Hello, Ranger.' He and Vinnie were smiling and acting very friendly, Josh noticed. He hoped that Logan wouldn't be fooled by them.

'How's the fishing?' said Logan, smiling.

'Slow,' said Russ.

'Too early in the day,' said Vinnie.

Logan's smile was suddenly gone. 'You know that you're not allowed to leave the trail with ATVs,' he said.

'Of course we know that, but my friend Russ here has a bad leg.' Vinnie gave a nervous little laugh.

'It's an old football injury,' said Russ.

'I'm sorry to hear that,' said Logan in a cool voice, 'but you know that the park has special fishing places for people with handicaps.' He gave the two of them a sharp look. 'Can I see your licenses?'

'Sure, Ranger,' Russ said with a big smile, and both of them pulled out their licenses and handed them to Logan. He studied the papers carefully. 'There's nothing here about a handicap,' he said finally, looking at Russ's license.

'It's - it's not exactly a handicap, Ranger. It, um, only gets bad once in a while.'

'Like today?' Logan said, poker-faced.

'I get the feeling you're making fun of my friend, Ranger,' said Vinnie, taking a step closer to him. 'You wouldn't want us to report that to your boss, would you?'

'I'm just doing my job,' said Logan. 'That's what my boss likes. So, yeah, go ahead and report it to him.'

'Well, we'll leave if that's what you want. But you haven't heard the last of this,' said Russ.

'You're forgetting something, aren't you?' The ranger studied the men's faces. When they didn't react, he said, 'What you did to the boy. First, you threw away his cell phone and took his camera chip, then you left him way up there,' he said, pointing towards the top of the hill above the stream. Those are criminal offenses. You'll have to come back to the station with us. After that, you can tell your story to the police.'

12 **handicap** ['hændɪkæp] a physical or mental disability – 13 **license** ['laɪsᵊns] an official document giving permission to use, own or do something. *(here:* to fish) – 21 **to make fun of sb** to laugh at sb, tease

For a long second, the two men stared at Logan with open mouths. Then they gave Josh a cold look. 'I don't know what the boy told you, Ranger, but I'm sure we can clear things up,' Vinnie said. 'Of course, we'll go with you.'

'I knew you would want to cooperate. Now the first thing is, when we go back out to the trail, I want you to drive slowly and follow me. I'll walk along the track you made when you drove in. That way there won't be any more damage to the woods,' Logan said in a sharp voice.

The two men nodded. Logan and Josh waited as they put away their fishing equipment. Suddenly, Vinnie turned around with a knife in his hand. 'Now you are the one who has to cooperate, Mr. Smart-Ass Ranger. And the first thing you're going to do is give us your cell phone.'

Logan hesitated, looking at the two men as if to say you can't be serious about this.

'Give - me - the - cell - fast!' Vinnie screamed, pointing the knife at Josh.

Logan reached in his pocket and handed over his cell phone.

Vinnie handed it to Russ and said, 'Now, Russ, tie our friends up!'

The older man took some rope from the box on his ATV and cut it in two pieces. He had just turned to face the ranger when he noticed that there was something in his hand.

'Vinnie! Watch out. He's got - 'Before he could say another word there was a Sssss sound like a snake. At the same moment, Vinnie dropped the knife and put his hands on his face. 'AGHHH!' he screamed. Russ jumped for the knife but before he got to it, Logan grabbed him and pushed him up against a tree. 'Pick up the knife, Josh,' he said. 'And you, dude, stay right where you are or I'll have to give you some of the same stuff I gave your partner.'

Russ stood very still.

Vinnie was in a state of panic. 'My face - it's on fire!' he screamed. He was jumping about like a break dancer. 'Don't rub your eyes!' Logan said. He handed Josh the can of pepper spray and told him to guard Russ while he took care of the younger man.

8 **sharp** sudden, angry – 35 **to take care of** to deal with

'Calm down!' he said to Vinnie. He took him by the hand and led him into the stream. 'Here. You can wash out your eyes now.'

Vinnie reached into the stream with both hands and threw the water onto his face. After a while he stopped screaming but a moment later, when he tried to open his eyes, he got a shock. 'I - I can't see! I can't see!'

'Relax,' said Logan. 'In a little while your eyes will be back to normal.'

A half hour later at the station, his eyes were red but he could see. He and Russ were sitting quietly, trying to follow the conversation in the next room.

'I don't think you should call them.'

'Are you sure? Think about what they did to you. You could have got lost up there on that hill, you know.'

'I know.'

'That's what they wanted. They wanted you to get lost.'

'Maybe.'

'Don't you think they deserve to be punished for that?'

'I think they've been punished enough. They've learned their lesson.'

There was a pause. Someone got up and started walking around.

'Vinnie pulled a knife on us.'

'I know.'

There was another pause, longer this time.

'You really want to do it this way?'

'I do.'

'That's really big-hearted of you, Josh. I don't think - if that had happened to me -

I don't think I could be so - so forgiving.'

'Hey, come on. It's not such a big deal. Besides, as I said, I think they've learned their lesson.'

No one spoke for a moment. Then: 'Okay, Josh, we'll do it your way. I hope they realize how lucky they are.'

In the other room, Vinnie looked at Russ with his swollen, red eyes, smiled and nodded his head. Russ nodded and smiled back.

30 **It's not such a big deal.** It's not very important.

7

Now that the summer vacation was at an end, Josh had much less time for the park, but he made the best of it. After getting home from school, he hurried there to get in an hour or so before supper. It wasn't the same as the almost unlimited time he'd had in the beautiful weeks gone by, but that short time was important to him, an oasis in the desert. And, thank God, he still had the weekends.

It was on one of those weekends that he met Bridget. He was approaching the Ranger Station when he heard voices. Through the open door, he saw a girl about his age talking with Ranger Logan. He didn't recognize her at first because of the baseball cap she was wearing. Then he realized it was Bridget Campbell, a girl he had seen at school. 'Hello,' he said softly as he entered the room.

'Hello, Josh,' said Logan with a big smile. 'I was just talking about you.' He put his arm behind the girl's back and led her over to Josh. 'You know Bridget, don't you? I told her that you're a good friend of mine - and a very good friend of the park.'

Josh's face grew warm. He smiled at Bridget and nodded. She smiled back.

'As you may know, Bridget is a reporter for your school newspaper and has come to me to get help with a story about the park. I was just telling her that I'd like to be of assistance but I don't really have the time. I said you might be able to help her with her story. I hope I'm not putting you on the spot.'

Josh smiled. He tried to answer but couldn't at first. He felt like - like a fish in a net. Bridget's smile was the net. 'I - uh - yeah - I'd be happy to help.' His face grew warmer. He hoped it wasn't as red as it felt.

'Hey, thanks,' she said, and her bright eyes seemed to grow brighter, 'you don't know how much this means to me.'

And you don't know how much it means to me, Josh thought.

Logan gave a little laugh and said, 'Well, I guess it's a good thing that I'm so busy. I think Josh is the right person for you to talk to. He loves the park and knows all about it. Now if you'll excuse me, I have to get back to my work.' He gave them a big smile and started to go to his desk but hesitated. 'Here, Josh.' He held out a card. 'Here's my cell number in case you need it.' Josh took it and thanked him.

The next thing Josh knew, Bridget had pulled a notebook and pencil out of her backpack and was looking at him expectantly.

'Whoa, Bridget, not so fast. First we have to decide what kind of story you want. You could write a thousand stories about the park. It's a world in itself. There is so much you could say about it, so many sides to it ... I think it's important to narrow the topic down, don't you?' Josh paused a moment. 'Or did you want to write a statistical-type article? You know, how high is the highest mountain in the park, how many trails are there, and stuff like that?'

'Of course not. Readers can get that kind of information in the

11 **to put someone on the spot** to make someone feel uncomfortable by asking a difficult question –
26 **expectantly** [ɪk'spektᵊntli] expecting him to do sth –

Internet. What I'm looking for is a special story, one you can't find on the Internet. Have you got any ideas?'

Josh thought for a moment. 'What about illegal camping?' he said.

'What's that?'

'It's camping against the park rules. It's off-limits camping, camping where camping isn't allowed – because of the danger to wildlife and vegetation.'

Bridget's eyes opened wide. 'But most campers stick to the rules, don't they?'

'True, most do. But, unfortunately, there are always a few who don't pay any attention to the rules. You'd be surprised at the things they do. Not only do they camp in areas where they aren't allowed to, they also cut down trees for firewood or worse - they use fences and signposts. Also, they leave behind all kinds of garbage - including human waste. Perhaps the worst thing of all is, they make fires during dry periods when campfires are not allowed and sometimes cause forest fires.'

'Bah!' There was anger in Bridget's voice. 'Can't the rangers catch those people?'

Josh shook his head. 'They catch maybe one in ten. Unfortunately, there are way too few rangers for this huge park.'

For a moment, Bridget was very thoughtful. Then she said quickly, 'That's the story I want! I think it's something our readers should know about. It's terrible!'

'I agree,' Josh said, nodding. 'Are you ready?'

'Ready!'

'Okay, let's get started! Our first stop will be the Great Bear Trail. It's not far from here. We can get there in an hour.'

'An hour?'

'Come on, Bridget. You want your story, don't you?'

'Of course I do.'

'Well, it's not going to come to you. You have to go out and get it.'

She laughed. 'You're the boss, Josh. Lead the way!'

16 **human waste** feces, solid material that leaves animals' bodies after digestion – 22 **way too few** much too small a number/too small a number by far

8

When they reached the Great Bear Trail Josh stopped and pointed at a sign. It read 'NO CAMPING ON POWDER RIVER'. He looked at Bridget. 'That's where we're heading for,' he said. 'Do you want to keep going or would you like to stop and take a break now?'

'I'm fine. Let's keep going.'

'Okay, but we have to leave the trail now and go through the woods. You see that river down there?'

Bridget's eyes followed the direction Josh was pointing in. 'Yeah,' she said.

'Well, that's it. That's the Powder River. People like to camp there. But as the sign says, it's a no-go area for campers.'

'Do we have to go through those deep woods?'

Josh gave a little laugh. 'It's the only way to get there - unless you've got a helicopter.' He reached in his pocket and pulled out a compass. 'Don't worry about getting lost. I've got this - and I know how to use it. As I said, if you want the story, you've got to go after it. It's out there in those woods. That's where the story is.'

'Right. Let's go!'

With Josh leading the way, they moved slowly through the thick woods. They had been walking half an hour when Josh suddenly turned to Bridget and smiled. 'Do you hear it?' he said. 'It's the sound of the river.'

Bridget put her hand to her ear and listened. 'Yeah. I can hear it!' There was excitement in her voice. 'It sounds really powerful.'

'It is. But we'll soon be there and you can see for yourself. Follow me!' Josh said and headed off in the direction of the sound.

A few minutes later, they came out of the woods and started across the riverbank. 'It's beautiful here!' Bridget cried. The river was deep with clear, fast-moving water and a wide, sandy bank.

'Now you know why people like to camp here,' Josh said in a flat voice.

Suddenly, Bridget became very thoughtful. 'What are we going to do if we see illegal campers?'

Now Josh became thoughtful, too. He looked out at the river for a moment, then turned to Bridget. 'A very good question. There are two types of illegal campers. There are those who know that what they're doing is wrong and who leave peacefully when spoken to. Most are like that, but then there are a few who feel they have the right to camp anywhere. They haven't got any respect for the park rules and what they mean. Those are the ones you have to be careful of. They can get nasty and aggressive sometimes.'

'Oh. They wouldn't do anything to us, would they?'

Josh's face grew serious. 'It can happen,' he said slowly, 'but I've learned how to deal with these people. When I see them getting aggressive I back off quickly. That's the best way. That way no one gets hurt.' Josh was thinking of what had happened to him at Little Joe's Stream but thought it best not to say anything about it.

Bridget looked at him with worried eyes. 'I hope we don't meet up with people like that.'

'If we do, I'll be careful. And I always have this with me.' He pulled out his cell phone and showed it to Bridget. 'I can call the Ranger Station if we get in trouble.'

'That makes me feel safer,' she said with a little smile.

'Good.' Josh was happy that she was smiling again. 'So let's get going. It's easy walking here along the bank.'

12 **to back off** to move away from

9

It was only a few minutes later when they came upon what had been a camp. It had been made, Josh said, maybe a week before. Litter lay all around: beer bottles, food wrappers, even an old pair of socks! He showed Bridget where the campers had made a fire.

Bridget shook her head sadly. 'I don't understand people who would do something like this,' she said.

'Crazy, isn't it? They spoil the very thing they come to enjoy. They have no consideration for others!' Josh said in a loud, angry voice. He took a bag out of his backpack and began to pick up the litter. Without being asked, Bridget began to help him. It was a magic

3 **wrapper** ['ræpɚ] piece of paper or plastic around food to keep it fresh or dry

moment for Josh. A warm feeling rose up inside him as he secretly watched her.

When they finished, he opened his backpack and pulled out a package. 'How about something to eat?' he said. Bridget nodded, and he gave her a sandwich. He pulled out another sandwich and a carton of chocolate milk and they sat down in the sand and began to eat.

'This campsite is nothing unusual. I've seen nine or ten like this one in the past few months.' He passed her the carton.

'Where?'

'Many of them were here, along the river.' He watched her as she took a long drink. 'The worst one was the one I found a couple of weeks ago. Besides all the litter, they had left several syringes behind. I was really afraid. One prick and I could have become very ill. I handled them with care, I can tell you.'

Bridget made a twisted face. 'That,' she said, 'is really gross.'

'Cookie?' Josh held out a handful of cookies.

'No thanks.'

'Oh, come on Bridget. Try one. My mom made them.'

She gave him a quick smile and took one. She took a bite and said, 'Mm. Very good.'

Josh looked at his watch. 'We should go back soon.'

'Oh, can't we go a little further? Just around the next bend?'

Josh hesitated but when he noticed the expectant look on Bridget's face he nodded. 'But only around the next bend. We'll take a quick look and then we'll have to go.'

Bridget smiled and gave his arm a little pat. 'Thanks, Josh,' she said.

13 **syringe** [sə'rɪndʒ] plastic or glass tube with a hollow needle used to inject drugs into the body – 14 **prick** a very small hole – 16 **gross** [grəʊs] very unpleasant – 27 **pat** soft, gentle touch on sb as a sign that you like them

10

Josh saw the smoke first. It was rising above the trees. Wordlessly, he turned to Bridget and pointed towards it. Then he continued on slowly. They were halfway around the bend when he heard voices. As he moved forward he kept close to the trees along the riverbank.

Suddenly, he stopped and put his finger to his lips. 'There they are,' he whispered. Bridget saw them at once. There were three people, two men and a woman. They were sitting around a campfire and talking. Behind them was a tent and behind that, half in the water, half on the bank, was a big white boat with a large motor.

'What are you going to do?' Bridget said softly.

'I'm going to talk to them. Would you rather stay here?'

'I'll come with you. A good reporter has to be where the action is.' She laughed softly.

With Bridget behind him, Josh moved out from behind the trees and walked slowly along the bank towards the campers. When the men saw the two of them coming, they stood up quickly. *Oh, oh,* Josh thought, *I don't like the way they're looking at us.* 'Hello,' he said, putting on a friendly smile.

'What do you want?' one of the men said. With his huge, heavily muscled body and small head he looked to Josh like The Incredible Hulk.

Josh fought back his fear. 'Nothing,' he said. 'We're just walking along the river.'

'Well, why don't you just walk on by - quickly,' Hulk said.

That was what Josh wanted to do, but at that moment he glanced back at Bridget.

When he saw how she was looking at him, he turned back to the men and said, 'We will. But there's something I want to tell you first.' The two men looked at each other, surprised. 'Yeah? What do you want to tell us?' Hulk said.

'Camping is not allowed on the river. Camping wild like this can disturb animals and damage vegetation. You know that, don't you?'

Hulk eyed him darkly. 'Who in hell do you think you are? Park

Ranger's Little Helper? What are you going to do about it, Ranger boy?' he said in a mocking voice.

'Nothing. But if you're smart, you'll do something about it.' He glanced back at Bridget again. Her eyes were open wide. She couldn't believe how cool he was.

'Like what?' Hulk said with a little smile on his face.

'Like take your tent down, clean up your campsite and leave.'

The two men looked at each other again. They said nothing.

'Think about it,' said Josh.

'We are,' Hulk said and gave a cruel laugh.

'Come on,' Josh said to Bridget. He walked by the men quickly but as Bridget was about to pass them, Hulk reached out and grabbed her. Josh heard a cry and spun around. Hulk had one huge hand over her mouth and the other around her waist.

'Let her go,' said the woman.

He gave her an angry look. 'Shut up, Doris! I'm the boss here!' he cried. His cold eyes turned to Josh. 'If you know what's good for your girlfriend, you'll keep on walking,' he said.

Josh stood perfectly still.

'Hey! Did you hear me? I said get moving and don't look back. We're going to keep your girlfriend for a while.'

Josh hesitated, but then realized he had no choice. As he turned to go he gave Bridget one last, long look - straight into her horrified eyes, to show her that he would do everything possible to rescue her.

'That's right. Go home to your mommy. Don't worry about your girlfriend. She'll be safe with us. We'll leave her where she can be found. But remember: if you send the rangers or the police after us, something bad will happen to her. Do you understand? SOMETHING BAD!'

2 **to mock** to laugh at – 14 **waist** [weɪst] middle part of a person's body (between the chest and the hips)

11

Ranger Logan was talking to a group of park visitors when his cell phone rang. He excused himself and took a few steps to one side. When he returned to the group several minutes later, he said that something important had come up and he'd have to leave them.

A few minutes later he was in his SUV racing towards the Great Bear Trail. His heart was racing, too. He had often thought of Josh and Bridget during the afternoon and wished that he had been able to go with them. The terrible news Josh told him on the phone made him feel responsible for what had happened. If only he had been there!

As soon as he reached the beginning of the Great Bear Trail he saw someone running in his direction. It was Josh! He got out of the SUV and hurried towards him.

Reaching him, he was shocked at the sight of the boy's white face. Josh was trying to say something, but he was out of breath.

'Take your time, Josh. Take your time.'

'I - I'm sorry. I shouldn't have put Bridget in danger! It's – it's all my fault.' Josh was close to tears and his voice shook as he told Logan what had happened. When he finished, he covered his face with his hands. 'I should have known better. I shouldn't have told the men to leave. What a dummy! Putting on a big show to impress Bridget. If I'd kept my big mouth shut, she'd be here with me now.' Josh paused to fight back his tears. 'It's - it's all my fault,' he repeated.

Logan put his hands on Josh's shoulders. 'Hey, come on! If it's anybody's fault, it's mine. I heard you and Bridget talking about illegal camping. I should have warned you to be very careful.' Logan paused, looking the boy in the eye. 'But let's not waste any more time playing the blame game. We've got to try to help Bridget. I called the police and informed them of everything you told me. You gave me a very good description of the three people and their boat. The police will be watching for them.' Without taking his eyes off Josh, Logan went on. 'On my way here, I tried to think of what we - you and I - could do on our own. I hit on the idea that maybe we should go upstream. Maybe they think the police won't search for them there because of the strong upstream current.' Again Logan paused. 'What do you think?'

'I think it's a good idea.'

'You didn't see how strong the motor was, did you?'

'I didn't. But I did notice that it was a large motor.'

'Okay. It's worth a try. Come on, we'll drive to Bradley's Bridge - it's nine or ten miles upstream from here.' Logan closed his eyes and concentrated a moment. 'It'll take us less than ten minutes to get there. You said you saw them last just after three o'clock. Well, it's ten to four right now. Assuming that their motor is strong enough to do ten miles per hour against the current, we could get there on time to see them before they pass the bridge.'

'If they're going that way,' Josh said, with emphasis on the 'if'.

'Right. If they're going that way.' Logan smiled nervously.

1 **upstream current** *here:* the flow of the river coming from its source

12

As they climbed down the bank beside the bridge, the scene in which Hulk had his huge hands around Bridget raced through Josh's mind. Her wide-open eyes were staring at him. 'Please, help me!' they seemed to be saying. *Hang on, Bridget, we're coming,* he said to himself. He hurried to catch up with Logan, who was almost running down the bank.

They reached the riverbank and looked up and down the river, as far as they could see. For several moments, they stood there, staring. Then Logan looked at his watch. 'We can't stay here much longer. We've got to go on to the next bridge.'

'Wait a moment!' Josh was staring at something floating down the river. It was still too far away to recognize what it was, but something

11 **to float** [floʊt] to sit on top of the water (opposite of *to sink*)

told Josh it was important. 'Look!' he cried, pointing upstream. 'Do you see what I see?'

Both of them fixed their eyes on a small, red object, which was twisting and turning in the current.

'It's a cap!' said Logan.

'Bridget's cap!' Josh let out a strange laugh, part joy and part fear.

'You sure?'

'Perfectly sure. It's her red baseball cap, the one she was wearing.'

Logan pulled out his cell phone and dialed quickly. 'Officer Brody? Scott Logan. The kidnappers went upstream. They'll be passing the bridge near Darby in less than twenty minutes. I'm at Bradley's Bridge. Yes, right away. I'll be there in about five minutes. I'll stay out of sight and wait for you. Right. Roger.'

Closing his cell, Logan turned and started running up the bank, Josh right behind him. As they drove off, Josh took a last look at the river hoping to see Bridget's cap once more, but it had gone by.

13

They reached the bridge less than five minutes later and climbed down the rocky bank to the water's edge. There, for what seemed to Josh like hours, they stood staring down the river. His eyes were on the river, but his mind kept sliding back to Bridget. Suddenly, he heard Logan take a deep breath and saw him point down the river.

Josh looked and saw the front end of a white boat - the boat - coming around a bend. It was about a hundred yards away.

'Quick, before they see us!' Logan cried and they moved back into the bushes.

Logan opened his cell phone and dialed quickly. 'Officer Brody? It's me again. I'm at the bridge. The boat is coming. Where are you? In five minutes? Hurry! Roger.'

'What if the police don't get here on time?' Josh asked.

'They'll have to drive further upstream and stop them there.'

Josh nodded. Neither he nor Logan said another word as they watched the boat move slowly up the river. But, moments later, when it suddenly turned in their direction, they looked at each other with wide-open eyes. 'Oh, my God!' Logan said. 'They're - coming - here!'

'What?'

'They're going to let Bridget out here - at the bridge!' Logan said softly.

'What can we do?' Josh whispered.

'Watch and hope for the best. There's nothing else we can do.'

Josh held his breath as the boat came closer. He could see Bridget clearly now. She was sitting at the front of the boat, beside the woman. Hulk was running the motor. When they reached land Hulk cut the motor and turned to Bridget. 'We're leaving you here, sweetie.' Noticing her frightened eyes, he let out a loud laugh. 'You'll be all right. There's a little town about a mile down the road from the bridge.'

Without saying a word, Bridget got up and stepped out of the boat. She was turning to go when Hulk shouted at her. 'Hey! Where's your cap? You were wearing a cap!'

29 **to cut** to turn off

'I put it in my backpack,' she said quickly.

Hulk eyed her for a moment. Suddenly, he jumped out of the boat and grabbed her by the arm. 'You tricked us, didn't you? You threw that damned cap in the river. To put the police on our trail!' He began to twist her arm. 'THAT'S WHAT YOU DID, DIDN'T YOU?' Bridget screamed in pain.

Josh went crazy with anger. Suddenly, he jumped out from behind the bushes. Hulk saw him coming. 'Well, well. It's Ranger's Little Helper again! Stop right where you are! If you come one step closer, dude, your girlfriend will need a new arm!' To show that he meant what he said, he twisted Bridget's arm until she cried out again. Josh stopped and stood very still. At that moment, Logan came out and stood beside the boy.

'Hey! What have we got here? A real ranger!' Hulk laughed. Then his face grew dark. 'You and your little friend here have got ten seconds to get the hell out of here. Ten - nine - eight - '

Logan was very calm. 'If I were you I'd hand over the girl and leave while you still can. The police will be here in a few minutes.' He looked Hulk straight in the eye. 'If you hurt her,' he said slowly, 'it'll only make things much worse for you.'

Hulk's mouth fell open. For a moment he was speechless, but then he exploded in anger. 'SHUT YOUR FACE, RANGER. I'M GIVING THE ORDERS HERE. I'LL SAY IT ONLY ONCE MORE: GET OUT OF HERE - FAST!'

'All right, all right, we're on our way. I just wanted to say one thing to the girl first, if that's okay with you.'

'Huh?' Unsure of how to react, Hulk turned his eyes to the other man to see what he thought of the Ranger's strange request. At that moment, Josh noticed Logan's hand move towards his back pocket. He knew what was coming.

'Bridget,' Logan said in a calm voice, 'CLOSE YOUR EYES!' Suddenly, like a snake striking, he jumped forward, his hand shot out and there was that Ssssss sound. Hulk let go of Bridget and jumped back but it was too late. The pepper spray hit him full in the face. Screaming with pain, he ran blindly towards the river but bumped into the boat and fell. His head hit a rock and he passed out.

Josh took Bridget's arm and pulled her aside. Without warning, the other man got out of the boat and came at Logan from behind. He pulled the ranger down and started hitting him. Josh hesitated a moment, then took off his backpack and hit the man over the head with it. The man turned and went after Josh. Logan got to his feet and tackled the man. For several moments, the two of them rolled back and forth in the sand. Finally, the man hit Logan hard and got up.

'Stay right where you are!' Bridget cried. She was holding the can of pepper spray in front of her. 'One wrong move and you get this in the face!'

'No, no, please!' said the man, holding up his hands.

'Don't move,' Josh told the man. Taking a piece of rope from the boat, he tied him up. Then he turned to Logan and helped him to his feet. Logan shook his head and looked around. Seeing Hulk still lying beside the boat, he got another piece of rope and tied him up, too. The woman in the boat got up. 'What are you going to do with me?' she said.

'Just stay where you are,' Logan said.

Josh took Bridget in his arms. He looked deeply into her eyes. 'Are you alright?' he said.

'I'm fine - except for my arm. I - I think it's broken.' She forced a little laugh.

'Let me look.' Josh took a step back and looked at her arm. It hung loosely by her side. Using his belt, he made a sling. Then, very gently, he put it around her neck and slipped her arm through it. 'How's that?' he asked.

'Better. Much better,' she said and gave him a smile that went through him like an electric shock - but much nicer.

'Hey, you guys! Sorry to break this up but the police are here.' Logan pointed towards the bridge. Josh looked up and saw that two police cars had arrived. He laughed. 'They'll be disappointed,' he

1 **to bump into** to hit sth hard – 1 **to pass out** to lose consciousness – 27 **sling** a support which people need when their arm is broken

said straight-faced. 'There's not much left for them to do.'

After the police had taken Hulk and the other two away, Logan talked with Josh and Bridget for a few minutes before following them up to the SUV. Watching the two of them, he couldn't help but notice the gentle way Josh was holding Bridget's hand as he helped her up the bank. A sad little smile crossed his face as he became aware that Josh maybe wouldn't be coming to the park in the near future. He would miss him. But a moment later his face brightened up again when he realized that, sooner or later, the boy would be back. Knowing him the way he did, Logan could be sure of that.

1 **straight-faced** [ˌstreɪt'feɪst] showing no sign of being amused in a funny situation

Answers to Quiz:

1 21.3 miles (34 kilometers)
2 397 miles (635 kilometers)
3 About 800,000 acres (3,237 km^2), about the size of the state of Rhode Island.
4 Mount Washington is 6,288 feet (1,916 meters). The world's highest mountain, Mount Everest is 8,848 meters high.
5 In no particular order: weasel, mink, raccoon, skunk, bobcat, fox, muskrat, deer, moose, black bear, opossum, hare, fisher, porcupine, coyote, squirrel, beaver, chipmunk, woodchuck, etc.
6 Over six million. Only the Great Smoky Mountains National Park has more (8-10 million).
7 23 campgrounds, some open year-round, most from mid-May to mid-October.
8 It starts in the state of Georgia and ends in the state of Maine.
9 The AT runs over 2,100 miles (3,360 kilometers), along the mountain range of the same name, through 13 states in the eastern United States.
10 1,200 miles of trails (1,900 kilometers)
11 Over 100 miles (160 kilometers)
12 There are 155, making up 8.5% of the total area of the U.S., an area almost twice the size of Germany.
13 The national forests can be used commercially, e.g. for timber harvesting or livestock grazing. The national parks cannot be used commercially.